Opening up Easter

Opening up Easter has been written in response to requests from teachers who found our publication *Christmas: A Year by Year Approach* supportive when planning a progression of learning in this key Christian festival. This book aims to support children and teachers in learning about and from the beliefs, events, customs and experience which make up the most significant festival in the Christian calendar, Easter.

This publication provides practical suggestions for helping children develop their knowledge and understanding of the events of Easter, the key beliefs and concepts underpinning the festival and the experience of Easter for Christians. Each of the units uses a variety of engaging pedagogies and practical learning activities to allow children to learn about and from the experience of Easter, enabling them to draw meaning from the festival for themselves.

Teachers often express concern about addressing some of the key ideas and events of Easter such as crucifixion, resurrection, sacrifice and salvation. The year-by-year approach allows these events and beliefs to be addressed in a progressive manner using engaging and thought-provoking activities.

For the subject leader we have provided a series of pages that can be shared with staff who are unsure about teaching Easter every year. These pages support subject leaders in teaching the festival accurately and appropriately, ensuring a progression of concepts through the primary school.

Fiona Moss
Editor

Web links: RE Today website

The RE Today website offers subscribers some free additional resources and classroom-ready materials related to this publication. Look out for the 'RE Today on the web' logo at the end of selected articles.

To access resources:

- go to the RE Today website www.retoday.org.uk

- click on the **download login** button and use the password from this term's issue of *REtoday* magazine

- click on **Primary curriculum publication – web supplement**

- click on the title of the publication and scroll down the page to find what you are looking for.

Contents

RE Today
Services

TEACHING EASTER ACROSS THE PRIMARY SCHOOL
planning for progression

For the teacher

Easter is the most important festival for all Christians. Many schools teach about Easter annually. This approach provides a good opportunity to look at this important festival in depth but requires careful planning to ensure children are provided with opportunities to build on earlier learning.

This book provides activities which support progression in learning about key concepts that are integral to understanding the festival and its importance to Christians. The grid below provides an overview of these learning opportunities.

An additional progression grid is offered on pages 30–1. This grid suggests additional learning opportunities and activities to those offered in detail in this publication.

Short television clips of the celebration of Easter in different traditions and the key parts of Easter week can be found in the BBC Learning Zone class clips library.

See: www.bbc.co.uk/learningzone/clips

The Easter story in the Bible

Event	Location in the Bible
Jesus' triumphant entry into Jerusalem	Luke 19:28-40
Throwing the moneychangers out of the temple	Luke 19:45-48
Sharing the bread and wine at the last supper	Luke 22:1-23
Judas betrays Jesus and Jesus is arrested	Luke 22:39-54
Peter denies Jesus	Luke 22:54-62
Jesus' trial	Luke 23:1-23
Crucifixion of Jesus	Luke 23:26-54
The empty tomb	Luke 24:1-12

Paige, aged 8, created this image for the NATRE Spirited Arts competition.

Year	Theme	Learning about Easter	Learning from Easter	Pages
R/1	Remembering Jesus	• Hearing and recreating elements of the Easter story • Listening to what Christians do to celebrate Easter	• Talk about times when they remember sad and happy times in their lives	3–7
1/2	Sorrow and joy	• Identify how music can reflect emotions and tell the story of Easter	• Talk about the positive and negative emotions that they experience	8–11
3	Hope from despair	• The importance of the idea of life after death for Christians	• Ask and answer some of their own questions about life after death	12–15
4	Sacrifice	• Understanding Christian beliefs about the crucifixion of Jesus	• Making links between the sacrifice of Jesus and Christian attitudes to serving others	16–19
5	An Easter experience	• Creating an Easter experience that shows what the Easter story means to Christians	• Reflect on why Easter matters to Christians and what matters to them	20–25
6	Resurrection and salvation	• The concepts at the heart of the Easter story: incarnation, forgiveness, hope, redemption, resurrection and salvation • The impact of Easter on the everyday life of practising Christians	• Reflect on the beliefs that are important and significant to them	26–29

RE Today Services

OPENING UP EASTER WITH YOUNGER CHILDREN

Remembering Jesus

In this section, Marilyn Bowles, an Early Years specialist from Leicester, shares nine strategies for introducing younger children to the Easter story and how this is remembered by Christians today.

Using art, role play, visitors and artefacts, these activities allow young children to begin to understand this most significant of Christian celebrations.

For the teacher

To appreciate the story of Easter, young children need to understand who the 'person' of Jesus is and to know that he: surrounded himself with friends, listened to people and was moved by their illnesses to heal them, both in body and mind. They need to know some of the stories he told – at this stage not necessarily what they meant as parables but the 'story-ness' of them which attracted the crowds when he spoke.

We need to avoid the situation where children know in great detail (because of countless Nativity rehearsals) much more about the story of Jesus' birth than they ever know about his life and teachings and the importance of his death and resurrection for Christians.

The Easter story has many complex parts to it – understanding a basic 'framework' of key events is the most appropriate strategy for young children. This information will eventually become extended and absorbed by children studying Christianity over several years: the Early Years is the beginning of this process – too much information, too soon is not necessarily helpful.

The key events of the story for young children are:

* Palm Sunday

* The Last Supper

* Jesus' arrest

* Good Friday

* The empty tomb on Easter Sunday.

There should be planned opportunities built in for children to ask their own questions about these events. This will reveal what they are thinking and whether they have an appreciation of what Christians might believe.

What can children do as a result of this unit?

These pupil-friendly 'I can . . .' statements describe what pupils working at levels 1 and 2 may achieve through this work.

Level	Description of achievement: I can. . .
1	• talk about something Christians do at Easter • respond to questions arising from the events of Easter • *talk about special days in my family.*
2	• think of some questions to ask a Christian • retell the story of Easter and say how Christians today celebrate Easter • *respond, with thoughts of my own, to ideas of new life in the story of Easter.*

See also

The Easter Story, Brian Wildsmith, OUP Oxford, ISBN 978-1-19272-377-2
This book retells the Easter story though the eyes of the donkey that carried Jesus to Jerusalem.

The Lion First Bible, Pat Alexander, Lion Hudson plc, ISBN 978-0-74596-103-3
More than 60 Bible stories are presented for young children, with bright illustrations and simple, clearly laid out text.

Festivals 2: Easter, Vaisakhi, Wesak and Christmas
This DVD by Child's Eye Media for 3–6 year olds follows young children and their families as they celebrate four festivals.
See: http://shop.retoday.org.uk

Telling the Easter Story
A PowerPoint supporting a simple telling of the Easter story, with well-drawn and provocative illustrations. The site provides many other images illustrating aspects of the life of Jesus.
See: www.sermons4kids.com/hmartin.htm

Cross-curricular links

* **Creative development:** drawing, working with small-world play and modelling materials

* **Literacy:** speaking; listening and responding; group discussion and interaction; drama (role play)

* **PSHCE:** working with others, discussing beliefs, values and practices, collaborating with others and developing respect and sensitivity.

Activity 1

Sharing the stories of Holy Week and Easter

You might try:

• Reading a version of the story, getting children to perform a set action when a particular name is mentioned, e.g. make 'clip clop' sounds when the donkey is mentioned; stand up and throw a fishing line when Peter is mentioned; do 'thumbs down' when Pilate is mentioned; make a cross with two fingers when Jesus' name occurs. This sets up for later consideration different people's actions in the story.

• Count and order all the different characters in the story. Have their names on flash cards to get the talking going.

• Use a Big Book, web-based or filmed version of the story in pictures to go with the telling of the story (e.g. 'Miraclemaker' or 'Animated Life of Jesus' from Channel 4 Learning).

• Ask children to choose their favourite moment, the saddest moment and the happiest moment from the story.

Activity 2

Visits and visitors

Inviting *real* **Christians** to talk to children in small groups is a very powerful way to interest children in the Easter story. A member of staff, a local church minister or an articulate child will be able to speak from real experience. Before Easter it is helpful to have met some real Christians and visited a place of Christian worship.

Visiting, looking at, touching artefacts in a **place of Christian worship** and seeing what Christians are doing there to celebrate Easter can be memorable.

When you invite a visitor in, identify a clear purpose such as sharing how a part of the Easter story is remembered at their church.

You could ask them to explain:

• palm crosses and a Palm Sunday procession

• their feelings when they are in a service on Good Friday, and play part of a song that might be sung

• the different mood in the service on Easter Sunday, and play some music that might be used in church.

Activity 3

Persona dolls

A **Christian persona doll**, who may have already told the children how s/he celebrated Christmas, can further be used to talk about what Christians believe. Learning why they go to church, how they study the Bible in Sunday School and pray at meal or bed times is an obvious strategy to use to explore the whole Easter story.

The children will eventually ask their own questions to help their understanding.

More on Persona Dolls from:

• *Persona Dolls in Religious Education* by Shahne Vickery, Jumping Fish, Diocese of Gloucester, ISBN 978-0-95566-112-9.

• *The Little Book of Persona Dolls* by Marilyn Bowles, Featherstone Education, ISBN 978-1-904187-86-8.

Lily, a Christian persona doll, shares the reasons why she goes to church at Easter with a group of Foundation Stage 2 children.

Speaking and listening to a member of the Salvation Army about her **Christian faith**

Speaking and listening to a member of staff about how her prayer beads help her pray

RE Today
Services

For the teacher

Sometimes RE with the youngest children doesn't get far beyond listening to a story. Here's a simple way of helping 4–5s think about 'what matters'. The activity is for after the children have heard the story of Jesus' last days, which can be from a book, a video or – best of all – told dramatically by a teacher.

Tell the story from Palm Sunday to Easter Sunday, including the Last Supper, and the crucifixion and resurrection.

You can do these activities with a whole class, but focus will be better if you do the tasks in small groups of 6–8 with an adult to talk to the children.

Early Learning Goals

The Early Learning Goals (ELGs) for creative development are practised through this activity, and its aims include developing problem solving and reasoning through talk (a part of the ELG for numeracy, which doesn't usually feature in RE).

As the creativity ELGs require, pupils will:

- **respond** in a variety of ways to what they see, hear, smell, touch and feel

- **express and communicate** their ideas, thoughts and feelings by using a widening range of methods.

 A simple PowerPoint supporting this work for the classroom is available to RE Today subscribers.

See: www.retoday.org.uk

Activity 4
What really matters at Holy Week and Easter?

These activities are to use once the story of Easter has been shared with the children.

Remember ten

- **Set up** a table or tray with ten items that are associated with Holy Week and Easter on it. My examples are: a hot cross bun, a chocolate egg, a cuddly toy rabbit, a daffodil, a palm cross, a crucifix and an empty cross, an Easter card, a glass of wine (or a small bottle) and a toy plastic donkey. Variations on this are possible.

Count and learn

- **Play** 'Kim's game': ask the children to look at the tray, then cover it and ask them if they can remember all ten things on the tray.

What links . . . ?

- **Ask** one child to suggest two of the objects that belong together, and say why: 'rabbit and donkey are both animals' / 'these two are both crosses' / 'bun and egg can both be eaten'. Give several children the chance to do this, and accept all answers – none is wrong here!

In the story . . .

- **Ask** if the children can say what each object has to do with the stories of Jesus that they have heard. If no one can connect one of the objects, then fill in the detail. Use the talk-time to reinforce details of the story and remind the group of key points.

Take away one by one

- **Discuss** with the children whether you can have Easter without these things. Talk about the different answers. It's probably true that without the cross, there is no Easter, so is the cross the most important thing?

Three reminders

- **Invite** children to choose three of the objects that they think are the best reminders of the story.

Most important?

- **Invite** them to say which of the objects might matter most to a Christian person, or might help them to remember Jesus' story.

- **Ask** pupils to use a paper template – a big circle divided into three is good – and make three drawings of the things that matter most at Easter. Give time to make this a beautiful piece of work. In small groups, children speak and listen about these pieces of work.

Links

- **Make some links** between the things that matter to Christians at Holy Week and Easter and the things, people and questions that matter most to them.

Activity 5
Timeline

It is important that the children understand that Jesus was not born and then died four months later.

- **Choose** some key stories from the life of Jesus that children will have heard and choose or create pictures of them.

- **Choose** at least five to share, such as a Nativity scene, Jesus as a boy at the temple, Jesus telling a parable, Jesus performing a healing and the death of Jesus.

- **Ask** children to place these in order on a timeline on the wall.

- **Alternatively** children could work in small groups discussing what the pictures show and then putting them in order.

Using the artwork can begin to put some order into the complexity of the plot!

Activity 6
Role play

Embedding and exploring the story of Jesus through **role play** can be very effective. Unearthing the Nativity wardrobe (minus kings' crowns and angels' wings!) can give the children opportunities to act out the stories they learn.

Clapping and singing for Palm Sunday – how would Jesus' friends have felt on:

- Palm Sunday
- Good Friday
- Easter morning
- When they saw Jesus again?

Activity 7
Retelling the story
Storytelling

Stories from different faiths need to be a regular part of the diet of stories (five-a-day!) that young children hear. Telling stories about Jesus (and other special people) from a wide variety of sources means that they are constantly being given opportunities to think and discuss new ideas. These opportunities need to be pounced on!

Any mention of chocolate, bunnies, bonnets or gardens dilutes the religious message and should be avoided in this context!

Small-world play / creative storytelling of aspects of the Easter story can embed the facts and raise questions for discussion.

Use figures and props to retell part of the story on a small scale. Different groups could use different props and materials to create three or four key parts of the story. For example:

- Small plastic figures showing Palm Sunday
- The Last Supper in plastic building bricks
- Playdough figures and scenery for the garden of Gethsemane
- Good Friday painted and the story retold
- The empty tomb created under a table

Each group could act as storytellers, as the class perform their own mystery play.

Activity 8
New life

A **spring 'walk of awareness'** is a lovely way to think about the new beginnings which Easter suggests: seeing how things are growing from seemingly dead earth.

Take the children to a local green space. It doesn't need to be a beautiful park – just an area where signs of new life in nature can be found. Then:

- **share** what each child found that is a sign of new life in nature

- **share** photos of other signs of new life in nature

- **ask**: did they find signs of bulbs, buds, leaves, flowers, baby animals, eggs and chicks?

- **give** each child a green leaf outline and ask them to choose what signs of new life they want to put on the leaf

- **make** a 'tree of new life' and hang on it all the leaves the children have made.

RE Today
Services

Activity 9

Remembering Jesus in church

Share with the children that for Christian families Easter is a really important festival and one of the ways that they remember Jesus is by doing special things at church

Ask:

- *What do Christians remember at Easter time?*
- *Do you celebrate a festival? What did you do?*
- *Do you do anything special at Easter time?*
- *Do you do anything to prepare for Easter?*
- *Do you do anything special on Good Friday or Easter Sunday?*

Show each of the pictures on the page, explaining what is happening and discussing the questions underneath the photographs.

Finally ask the children to draw a picture of the day they think is most important for Christians.

More able children will be able to say or write.

I think this day is the most important of the celebration of Easter because . . .

Palm Sunday

In many churches there is a joyful procession on Palm Sunday.

Why has Sam got a palm cross?

Palm Sunday was a happy day for Jesus and his followers, so why do you think Sam looks sad here?

Good Friday

What is Sam looking at?

Why do you think these objects are important at Easter time?

What does the cross and crown of thorns remind Sam of?

How do you think Sam might feel on this day? Why?

Maundy Thursday

Why do you think Sam is having his feet washed?

How do you think it feels to have your feet washed by someone else?

Which part of the story will this remind Sam of?

Children could wash each other's hands to see what this feels like.

 A simple PowerPoint supporting this work for the classroom is available to RE Today subscribers

See: www.retoday.org.uk

Easter Sunday

Many Christians get up early on Easter Sunday morning and celebrate a service at sunrise. Others take part in service full of joy later on Easter Sunday morning.

How do you think Sam might feel on Easter Sunday morning?

How have his feelings changed during this week?

RE Today
Services

SORROW AND JOY: USING SPIRITUAL MUSIC

For the teacher

Holy Week and Easter: what do they celebrate? Answers might include life from death, hope from despair, joy from sorrow, the victory of love over hate.

The next four-page section of the book provides you with four activities that enable children 5–7 years of age to connect up their own ideas and experiences to key elements of the stories of Holy Week and Easter.

These activities use some music, and we have been specific in suggesting examples – but you could easily use other examples of the music of Christian worship and celebration.

The simplest emotional language to use with younger children is to talk about sadness and happiness, but it is good to make progress in using emotional language that is more varied and descriptive than 'happy/sad' allows for. So try to get all children to think about sorrow/joy as well, and some children to use a wide and varied emotional vocabulary to describe the feelings of characters in the stories and their own feelings.

Activity I

Happy face, sad face

Give children a face outline copied from this example.

Ask pupils to:

• **Turn it** into either a happy face, or a sad face. It is drawn to work both ways!

• Use the face to **respond** to different parts of the stories as they are told.

Tell the children that the stories of Holy Week and Easter are special or holy for Christian people because they are about turning sadness to happiness, or turning sorrow to joy.

Questions of wonder

When pupils have made their face 'happy or sad', get them to **talk** by asking questions of wonder like these:

• I wonder – can anyone think of what makes us turn from sadness to happiness?

• I wonder – why it is hard to turn from sadness to happiness?

• I wonder – can anyone talk about how the Easter story turned the disciples' feelings upside down?

What can children do as a result of this unit?

These pupil-friendly 'I can . . .' statements describe what pupils working at levels 1, 2 and 3 may achieve through this work.

Level	Description of achievement: I can. . .
1	• name some people in the Easter stories • recognise how they felt in the stories • *talk about the feelings that go with the stories.*
2	• retell a part of an Easter story • identify some music that makes people happy, joyful, sad or sorrowful • *respond sensitively to stories, characters and emotions.*
3	• describe how Christians use music at Easter • describe what Christians believe about Jesus coming back from the dead • *make links between my experiences and feelings and those found in the stories of Holy Week and Easter.*

RE Today Services

Activity 2

Music for Holy Week and Easter: 'swirly patterns'

Christians make music for celebration. In this work, you will ideally need four pieces of music that express the story of Easter. Here, we suggest using two famous classical pieces, and two modern Christian children's songs. Other possible music is suggested in the Spirited Music section of the NATRE website. It is good to connect with learning in the Music curriculum in this work, and to use both child-friendly and more challenging music.

See: www.natre.org.uk.

Ask the children to:

- **Think** of the music that they like to hear when they are happy and when they are sad.

- **Talk about** any music that can make them happier when they are sad. Ask them to say why.

Play them these four items, one by one. While they **listen** ask the children to:

- **Create** four 'swirly patterns' on paper, to go with the music. The patterns should be made in colours and shapes that fit the mood of the music.

The songs last only about 3–4 minutes each, and this activity is good for concentration.

'Woah, He is Alive' by Stephen Fischbacher, from the CD *Something Fischy* 2000: www.fischy.com

Our friend is gone, we saw him die
Our friend is gone, we heard him cry
After all we've been through,
What are we supposed to do?

Our friend is gone, we feel ashamed
We ran away when the soldiers came
After all we've been through,
What are we supposed to do?

Oh, Let us in! Oh, Let us in!
You won't believe it – we don't believe it –
Will you listen: He is alive!

© Fischy Music, reprinted with permission

To discuss:

- What parts of the Easter story is the song about?

- How does the music show that the song changes sadness into happiness?

'Down to Earth' by Stephen Fischbacher, from the CD *Down to Earth,* 2009: www.fischy.com

He could have been born in a royal palace and called 'Your majesty', worn a crown of diamonds and lived in luxury,
but he was born in a dirty stable and laid on a bed of hay,
not too many welcomed him on the very first Christmas Day
CHORUS: He is down to earth.
The one who changed the world forever is down to earth.

He could have been friends with rich and famous with big celebrities, had anything he wanted, living as he pleased,
but he made friends with the poor folks, with the sick and with the lame,
he helped them with their problems and he called them all by name.

He could have been full of his importance, and felt so very grand his servants would have bowed and said 'Your wish is my command' but he wore a crown of thorns, gave everything he had he gave his life that we might know the great love of his dad.

© Fischy Music, reprinted with permission

To discuss:

- This song is about the whole of Jesus' life. What does the person who wrote it like about Jesus?

- Do you know any stories of Jesus that show he was 'down to earth?'

'The Crucifixion' by John Stainer

For God so loved the world that he gave his only Son, that whoever believes in him should not perish but have eternal life. For God sent the Son into the world, not to condemn the world, but that the world might be saved through him.

Bible, *Revised Standard Version*

To discuss:

- This song is about the Christian belief that Jesus died to save the world. What would you like to ask about this?

- What words describe the mood of the music?

There is a version of this oratorio by the St Paul's Cathedral Choir at www.youtube.com/watch?v=X5Akz6J8Rw0 It lasts for about 3 ½ minutes.

'The Hallelujah Chorus' from *The Messiah*, by G F Handel

Hallelujah, Hallelujah
For the Lord God Omnipotent Reigneth.
The kingdom of this world is become the kingdom of our Lord and of His Christ, and he shall reign for ever and ever.
King of kings and lord of lords for ever and ever. Hallelujah.

To discuss:

- This very famous song uses old fashioned language, but is full of joy. What mood do you think goes with the music?

- Do you like the word 'Hallelujah'? It means 'Praise the Lord' in Hebrew.

There's a useful four-minute version free at: www.youtube.com/watch?v=xdRyNea19PE&feature=fvw There are lots of versions to choose from.

Activity 3

Getting creative with the story

- **Set up** creative activities linked to the story's characters. Use artefacts of Easter. These may be borrowed from, or seen at, a local church, or use pictures from an artefacts website, or some drawn by pupils. You could include crosses and crucifixes, bread and wine and an Easter Garden.

- **Draw** around the children in suitable poses for Palm Sunday, the argument with the moneychangers, the Last Supper or the empty tomb on large sheets of paper, then paint them for a wall display. Make the creative work an exciting focus on new life.

- **Talk** in circle time about the words 'sorry' and 'forgive'. Why are these important words? In the story, there are lots of people who should have not done the things they did. Tell children about what Jesus said when he was crucified: 'Father, forgive them, they don't know what they are doing'. Is it true that, when someone forgives you, you can make a fresh start?

- **Talk** about Easter being a special event for Christians to celebrate Jesus rising from the grave. Use artefacts, video or pictures to show what happens in church on Easter Day.

- **Discuss** the turn-around in the story: hot cross buns are symbols for 'Good Friday', a reminder of the cross, but the symbols of Easter Sunday are all about new life.

Activity 4

Responding to the story

Choose one or two activities from below:

- **sequence** pictures or simple sentences

- **organise** children to produce artworks depicting the sequence of events in the Holy Week and Easter narrative

- **decorate** some leaves for a tree with some key moments from the story

- **write** the story in 30 simple sentences and give each child one sentence to illustrate, then create a 30-page class book of the story in the children's pictures (this makes a lovely display for Easter for a church to which your school has a link)

- **share** the story and act out the suggested feelings of the character e.g. who might have felt these feelings? Can the children make the faces? Frightened, shocked, happy, surprised, tearful, excited, joyous, proud, thrilled, amazed.

 A PowerPoint supporting this work for the classroom is available to RE Today subscribers.
See: www.retoday.org.uk

The Easter story in six scenes

Children work in groups of three. Give each group a six-page booklet to make six drawings in. You could pre-print simple outlines of the story onto facing pages, and get children to draw their own story book for Easter.

Stimulate their responses by sharing these six parts of the story:

- Listen to the **Palm Sunday** story: Jesus is welcomed by excited crowds, riding a young donkey. Talk about how people felt, why people loved Jesus, what the occasion was like. **Luke 19:28-40**

- Read/tell the story of **Jesus and the moneychangers in the temple**. Talk about what makes us angry, and why this made Jesus angry. Did it help Jesus to make friends, or make enemies? Is it sometimes OK to be angry? **Luke 19: 45-48**

- Next, take the story of **Jesus' last supper** with his disciples. Children might look at bread and wine, and spend a two-minute time of silence thinking about the story and its meaning. **Luke 22: 1-23**

- The fourth part of the story is about **Jesus' arrest and trial**. Children might hear about Judas who betrayed Jesus and the crown of thorns the soldiers used to mock him. Talk about the unfairness of these events. Do the children have examples of very unfair experiences? **Luke 23:1-23**

- The fifth section is the **crucifixion of Jesus.** Use some carefully chosen images to talk about this. The story is well told in the Channel 4 Animated Bible Story on the Life of Jesus in the 'Stop, Look, Listen' series 2005, product code 400817. Talk about the people who cried, and times when we cry. Consider why the Christians call this day 'Good Friday'. **Luke 23:26-54**

- The story of the **empty tomb** brings a happy ending to the story. Talk about why Christians believe in heaven and life after death. Why is this a story of hope? You might emphasise the way the music and songs have portrayed sadness and sorrow changing to joy and hope. **Luke 24: 1-12**

 RE Today Services

Activity 6 Emotions

1 Draw faces for these six emotions.
2 Think of times when you have felt these six emotions.
3 Think of the feelings people had in the stories of Holy Week and Easter.

Excited		Excited
Worried		Worried
Mystified		Mystified
Cross		Cross
Very upset		Very upset
Amazed		Amazed

RE Today
Services

For the teacher

This unit provides some suggestions for getting to the heart of the meaning of Easter for Christians. It explores with pupils the fact that at a human level the death of Jesus was extremely sad, but that Jesus' followers and Christians today believe it is a sign of hope.

The activities do not avoid the fact that at the centre of the story of Easter there is **death**. The ideas provided draw on a **variety of resources and stimuli** to support pupils' **understanding** of the hope provided for Christians by their belief in the **death and resurrection of Jesus**.

Information file

The empty cross reminds Christians of the resurrection of Jesus and the promise they believe they have been given that when they die they will be with God.

The crucifix, a cross with the body of Jesus on it, is more often used by Catholic and Orthodox Christians; it is a reminder of the sacrificial nature of Jesus' death.

There are many different types of crosses and crucifixes that can be used with pupils. Pictures and descriptions of many of them can be found on the internet.

See: www.strath.ac.uk/curricularstudies/re/db/reartefacts/christian

Cross-curricular links

Social and emotional aspects of learning

Ideas around death and loss are taught through the SEAL theme 'Relationships'.

Note:

- resources for teacher discussion can be found in 'Staffroom activities' (purple set)

- resources for Year 3 on the theme of loss can be found in 'Relationships' (yellow set).

Literacy

Skills of hot seating and the suggested poetry framework on page 13 could support work in Year 3 Unit 1: Poems to perform.

See: http://nationalstrategies.standards.dcsf.gov.uk

What can children do as a result of this unit?

The following pupil-friendly 'I can . . .' statements describe the learning that may be expected of pupils.

Level	Description of achievement: I can. . .
2	• suggest what the story of Easter might mean to a Christian today
	• *ask some questions about what happens when we die.*
3	• make a link between the death of Jesus and some key Christian beliefs
	• *ask some questions of my own about life after death, and suggest two different answers to each one.*

RE Today subscribers can also download the following from the RE Today website:

- Colour versions of the story and illustrations of Grubby Grub on page 15

- Colour copies of the eight crosses on page 14

- A photocopiable sheet of crosses for Activity 1

- A PowerPoint presentation to stimulate poetry writing.

See: www.retoday.org.uk

RE Today
Services

Activity 1

Friday crosses and Sunday crosses

Show the pupils a selection of crosses and crucifixes. You can photocopy sets of the eight images on page 14 to allow pupils to study them in groups or create your own selection of crosses for the pupils to handle.

- **Explain** that some Christians choose to wear or display a plain cross because they want to focus on the resurrection of Jesus, whereas other Christians choose to use a crucifix to focus on the pain Jesus suffered when he died.
- **Ask** the pupils to choose a cross that they like and **respond** to the two sentence starters on the cross outline on page 14.

Activity 2

Grubby Grub: using story to explore the idea of life after death

Read the story on page15 and share the illustrations with the pupils. After some discussion, give each group one of the questions below, in the centre of a large piece of paper. Ask them to discuss the questions and write down any ideas they have. The questions are then moved on until each group has discussed and responded to each question.

- Why might Christian people like this story?
- What might this story mean to people who believe in life after death?
- What do you believe about life beyond this life?
- When someone dies we are often very sad. What helps people get over their sadness? What might help Christians get over their sadness?
- What might this story tell us about Easter? Jesus?

Draw together the responses from the pupils.

Activity 3

Hot seating Mary

Explain to the pupils that they are going to receive a visit from Mary, the mother of Jesus. She is coming to visit them just after she has seen her son, Jesus, die on the cross.

1 **Share** a good Children's Bible or retelling of the death of Jesus on Good Friday. **See:** Luke 23:13-25, 32-48.

2 **Ask** the pupils to work in pairs to **devise** three questions to ask Mary.

3 Either the teacher or another willing adult takes the role of Mary, the mother of Jesus and the children **'hotseat'** Mary.

4 **Read** an extract from the Bible showing the women finding the stone rolled away from the tomb. **See:** Luke 24 1-12.

5 The pupils work in pairs again to **devise** three questions to ask Mary when she comes to visit them on Easter Sunday.

Activity 4

Responding through poetry

All the activities in this unit have explored the despair at the point of the death of Jesus and then the joy when there is understanding by Mary and of Christians today that the resurrection of Jesus brings hope.

- Pupils should use one of the two writing frames shown in the box at the top of this page to show their understanding of the change in ideas, feeling and beliefs between Good Friday and Easter Sunday that was experienced by followers of Jesus 2000 years ago and Christians now.

Sample poetry frames for Activity 4

Writing frame 1

On Friday there was . . .
Sunday brings . . .
Live . . .
On Friday there was . . .
Sunday brings . . .
Hope . . .
On Friday there was . . .
Sunday brings . . .
Think . . .
On Friday there was . . .
Sunday brings . . .
Believe . . .

Writing frame 2

Good Friday
What did he think when he . . .
He must have . . .
What do you think?

What did Mary think when he . . .
She must have . . .
What do you think?

Easter Sunday
What did he think when he . . .
He must have . . .
What do you think?

What did Mary think when he . . .
She must have . . .
What do you think?

RE Today
Services

SELECTION OF CROSSES

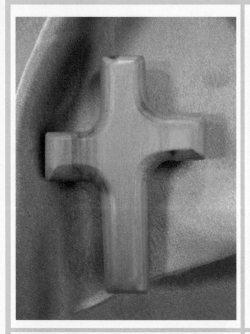

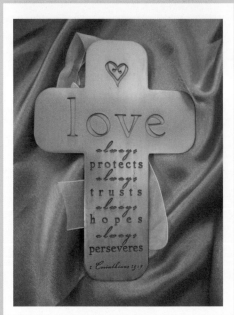

love
always
protects
always
trusts
always
hopes
always
perseveres

I like this cross because . . .

I think this cross shows . . .

RE Today
Services

Grubby Grub

Grubby Grub lived at the bottom of a deep pond. He was called Grubby Grub because he lay in the mud all day and hardly moved. He looked just like a twig with stones and sand on either side. All the other pond creatures were very fond of him and also very sorry for him. They could swim around the pond wherever they liked. They could go down to the thick weeds or right to the very top where the sunlight shone on the surface of the water. But poor Grubby Grub could only sit in the mud at the bottom of the pond.

'Poor Grubby Grub,' they used to say, 'he'll have to stay in the mud all his life.'

'He could climb up a stalk if he wanted to,' said a tadpole.

'Oh no,' replied a minnow, 'he'd get stuck, or fall off. Anyway he might go too near the top and we all know it is dangerous near the top. We don't want him to die.' The pond creatures started to get hungry and swam off to look for food.

Then, one day they had a surprise.

'Look at Grubby Grub,' the minnow said, 'he's climbing up the stalk.' And there he was. There was Grubby Grub climbing up the stalk. Very, very slowly, he moved towards the top. Everyone watched him in silence.

'He's getting too near the top,' said the tadpole, 'we'd better warn him. He will die if he gets to the surface.' They all started shouting: 'Stop Grubby Grub! Stop! You'll die if you get to the top.'

Grubby Grub took no notice. He climbed and he climbed and he climbed. At last he got to the very top of the pond. He poked his face above the water and crawled onto a large green leaf. He lay tired and happy in the warm sunshine. As he lay there, he suddenly felt his skin crack - it split all the way down his back. Grubby Grub wriggled out of his old skin and, after resting a little, he crawled to the edge of the leaf and looked down into the pond. In the reflection, he saw a creature with two beautiful white wings. He had changed into a Caddis fly. He could fly and explore the world – and what a world! The world was full of brilliant colours and wonderful smells. Grubby Grub thought:

'I'll go back and tell the pond creatures how wonderful it is here and that I'm not dead at all.' So he flew down to the pond. But, try as he might, he could not get into the water to tell the others what a beautiful place he had found.

Meanwhile back in the pond, the creatures had been anxiously waiting for Grubby Grub to return. As he had burst out of his old skin, the case had fallen into the pond and sunk down to the bottom. The pond creatures looked at each other in dismay,

'We told him he'd die,' they said sadly, 'now all that's left of him is an empty case.'

By Jane Brooke, adapted from
Waterbugs and Dragonflies
by Doris Stickney

Illustrations by Sarah Berry

WAS THE CRUCIFIXION OF JESUS A SACRIFICE?

What does it mean to Christians?

For the teacher

This unit explores the idea of **sacrifice** in relation to **Christian beliefs about Jesus' crucifixion**. It offers four ways in which Christians view Jesus' death as a form of sacrifice, giving pupils a 'way in' to understanding the significance of Jesus' actions for believers today.

The unit allows pupils to empathise with characters in four scenarios as a way in to understanding how Christians respond to Jesus. By applying each of these scenarios to ways in which Christians often see Jesus as their rescuer, pupils **make a link** with the **key Christian concepts** of **sin** and **atonement**. Pupils are given a selection of Christian views to help them express their understanding of Christian ideas about Jesus' death, and so that they can consider why Christians respond to Jesus with worship and devotion.

What can children do as a result of this unit?

The following pupil friendly 'I can . . .' statements describe the learning that may be expected of pupils.

Level	Description of achievement: I can. . .
3	• make links between Christian beliefs about Jesus as the 'Lamb of God' and ideas about Jesus' death as a sacrifice
	• *make links between the idea of sacrifice and my own attitude to putting others first, or serving others.*
4	• show understanding of Christian beliefs about Jesus' death as a sacrifice and the idea of him as the Lamb of God
	• describe how these beliefs have an impact on the lives of some Christians
	• *apply the ideas of sacrifice and forgiveness to my own life, comparing my views with Christian responses.*

Classroom activities

Activity 1   Setting the scene – four perspectives

Page 17 offers four scenarios to discuss in the classroom. This might be done through whole class talk, or you could put the scenarios on large pieces of paper around the room, and ask pupils to write their comments on sticky notes. A group could then take a sheet and report back.

Following discussion of the scenarios, ask pupils to explain in what way Joshua has sacrificed himself. Point out that Joshua is the modern version of Jesus' name – which is Yeshua in Aramaic, the language Jesus spoke. Yeshua means 'he saves'. How did Joshua 'save' people in the scenarios?

Activities 2–5   Why did Jesus die?

Take the information on page 18. Different groups could complete different activities and report back, or the activities could be experienced on a carousel. It might be helpful to talk through the 'taking someone's place' activity as a whole class. Some teachers might ask pupils to draw a symbol on a piece of paper to represent something they have done and are sorry about, and then shred the paper or, health and safety allowing, take the papers outside and burn them.

Activity 6   What difference does Jesus' sacrifice make to Christians?

Page 19 gives pupils a chance to make connections between the scenarios and Christian belief in Jesus as the sacrificial Lamb of God. Using the quotations from some young Christians, along with the discussion work and the activities from pages 17–18, pupils should write a short piece explaining Christian beliefs about sacrifice and their own responses.

RE Today
Services

A   Bearing a burden

Tom is carrying a rucksack. It is heavy and he cannot take it off. He feels as if he has been carrying it for ever. The straps dig into his shoulders and the heavy bag gets in the way as he goes through the day.

Talk about:

- How would Tom feel?
- What would it be like to carry such a burden?
- What would he like to happen?

Act out:

- Imagine you have this burden; what is it like to be weighed down?

One day, along comes Joshua. He offers to take the rucksack, if Tom would like.

Talk about:

- How does Tom feel about the idea of getting rid of the bag?
- What does Tom say?
- How does it feel to have the weight lifted off? How does Tom feel towards Joshua?
- What might he do in response?
- What words might you use to describe what Joshua has done?

B   Stepping in

Rachel is walking to school one cold winter morning, when there is a terrible accident. A car starts skidding on some ice, heading straight for her.

Talk about:

- In that instant, how does Rachel feel?
- What does she fear?
- What does she hope for?

Just then, Joshua, who was walking a few steps behind her, dives forward and pushes Rachel out of the path of the oncoming car. The car hits Joshua instead. An ambulance is called. Joshua is taken to hospital with serious injuries. A few days later, Rachel visits Joshua in hospital.

Talk about:

- Why would Joshua do such a thing?
- How might Rachel feel about what has happened? What could Rachel do to show her gratitude?

C   Lost

Imagine you're on holiday with some friends and have gone walking alone in some woods one afternoon. It's peaceful and calm as you walk deeper into the woods. Gradually, as the sun goes down and the shadows lengthen, you realise that you don't know where you are.

Talk about:

- Have you experienced being lost?
- How did you feel?
- What thoughts might go through your mind in the story above?
- What sights and sounds would you experience as darkness falls?

As the hours go by and your panic increases, the light goes and you are left in darkness. Eventually you hear a voice calling your name and a light through the trees. You call out and the light comes towards you. It is one of your friends, Joshua, who has been out searching for you and who knows the way back out of the wood.

Talk about:

- How would you describe the moment you heard the voice, then saw the torch light, then saw your friend coming towards you?
- What might the two of you say to each other?

D   Taking someone's place

Sam is in trouble! After messing about with some friends, Sam has broken a window at school. The only problem is, Sam is often in trouble and this is the latest in the long line of such accidents. This might be the last straw – perhaps Sam will face serious punishment now.

Talk about:

- How does it feel when someone knows they've done wrong?
- What if they have let someone they respect down and know they have to face the consequences? How does it feel when someone knows they deserve to be punished, and that this time it's serious?

As Sam realises that it is time to face the head teacher and take the punishment, Joshua, a friend who was nearby, offers to take Sam's place. Joshua is prepared to go to the head teacher and take the blame, taking the punishment and letting Sam go free this time.

Talk about:

- Why might Joshua be prepared to take the blame?
- Would Sam accept the offer?
- If Sam accepts, how might Sam respond to Joshua afterwards?

RE Today
Services

Bearing a burden

Christians generally see sin as a burden. When they don't have the right attitude to God or to others, or if they act selfishly, they often feel guilty. They want to be good but don't always manage it. They believe that Jesus will take the burden away if they ask him for forgiveness.

In groups, think of how to act out and present two freeze-frame images

- one to express how a Christian might feel when he or she has upset God

- one showing how he or she might feel after those sins have been forgiven.

Lost

Jesus told a story about God being like a shepherd who searches for a lost sheep (Luke 15:1-7). He also described himself as a good shepherd, prepared to lay down his life for his flock, and leading his people to safety (John 10:11-16). Christians also believe that Jesus does not just show them the way to heaven, he actually *is* the way. Through Jesus' sacrifice, he opens the way to heaven. Some Christians say Jesus is like a bridge carrying people from death to life.

Individually or in pairs, produce a piece of artwork that expresses the idea of being lost and then found.

- You might do a collage, using colours and images symbolically.

- Write a short paragraph explaining your picture and how it links to Christian beliefs about Jesus.

Stepping in

Most Christians do not see the Bible as full of loads of rules they have to obey. They believe that God loves them and that Jesus saves them from a terrible fate – life without God after they die. They want to please Jesus and thank him for his sacrifice on the cross – which makes it easier to follow Jesus' teachings. They also believe that following Jesus' teachings is what will make them get the most out of life.

In pairs, look at the list of Jesus' teachings, below

- Come up with an example of an occasion when it would be really difficult to follow this teaching.

- Take one and draw a short storyboard showing how a Christian might remember Jesus to help him/her do the right thing.

Do not boast
Love your enemies
Do not get angry
Don't worry about what will happen tomorrow
Do not spend all your time gathering up riches for yourself
If someone is ill, look after them.

Taking someone's place

Christians believe that in the Old Testament, God arranged to deal with people's sins through sacrifice. An animal – sometimes a lamb – was offered. The worshipper said sorry for his sins, and put his hand on the lamb, a symbol for transferring the sins onto the lamb. The lamb was then killed and the body burned on the altar. The worshipper's sins were gone! It was as if the lamb had taken the punishment for the worshipper. They were now at one with God again.

Imagine what it would be like to be able to take all the wrong things you have ever done or said, or even thought, and to put them onto paper and then burn the paper. As the flames lick upwards, the paper turns black and crumples, the writing disappears, leaving smoke and ash. All those wrong things have disappeared!

- How would it feel?

- Why might someone be happy with this?

Now find a copy of the picture *Agnus Dei* by Zurbaran. In pairs, try and work out why Christians call Jesus the 'Lamb of God'. http://www.jesuswalk.com/lamb/images/zurbaran-agnus-dei-lamb-of-god-madrid-1339x800.jpg

RE Today
Services

Activity 6   What difference does Jesus' sacrifice make to Christians?

Read the following comments from some young Christians.

• Take some sentence starters to help you write a short piece about the idea of Jesus' death as a sacrifice.

• Choose at least four sentence starters, and at least one from each box.

> When I have done something wrong and I ask Jesus to forgive me, I feel like a weight has been lifted from me.
> Dan, 13

> As a Christian I don't feel like I have a load of rules to follow. I want to be more like Jesus. When I'm close to him is when I feel best.
> Lois, 12

> When I think about Jesus dying it makes me wonder why he was prepared to die for me. I say sorry and thank you every day.
> Jacob, 14

> Jesus' death is horrible but it shows how much he loves people. I would have to love someone a lot to be happy to die for them.
> Aimee, 12

According to Christians the problem for human beings is that . . .	**Christians describe how they feel about Jesus by saying . . .**	**I agree with this because . . .**
		I disagree with this because . . .
Christians believe that sin . . .	**If Christians really believe this I think that they would . . .**	**I do/do not think that forgiveness is important because . . .**
Christians believe that Jesus' death was a sacrifice because . . .	**I would like to ask a Christian . . .**	**One thing I have learned about Jesus from this unit is . . .**
Christians call Jesus the Lamb of God because . . .	**I can see why Christians might devote their lives to Jesus because . . .**	**I would like to think a bit more about . . .**
When explaining the idea of sacrifice, Christians might say . . .	**If more people tried to help others then . . .**	**I am not sure about . . .**

Unpacking Easter

For the teacher

The lesson ideas in this section are designed to help children age 7–10 years to understand what the Easter story means to Christians. Through creating the activities or participating in the Easter experience created they will have opportunities to **make links** between their own lives and the message of the Easter story.

An Easter experience can be suitable to use in both a community school and a school with a religious character.

The activities and resources in this section can be used in two ways:

- **Children aged 9–10 years create** an Easter learning experience for either 7–9 year olds or parents to experience. This needs Activities 1–3 described on the opposite page.
- **Teachers create** a labyrinth for 9–10 year olds to participate in. This needs alternative Activity 4.

Constructing and leading the experience or 'labyrinth' or taking part in it will both inform pupils about Easter and also give space for a personal spiritual response. In a community school, opportunities for spiritual development can be overlooked and yet spiritual, moral, social and cultural development is a key purpose of education.

Resources

1 Pictures of Easter week
The full colour pictures on page 22 are available as free downloads for subscribers to RE Today.
See: www.retoday.org.uk

2 Pictures of the life of Jesus
This website has pictures and PowerPoint sequences illustrating the Easter story and other Bible stories.
See: www.sermons4kids.com/hmartin.htm

3 Story and pictures of Holy Week
This website has a short retelling of the story of Holy Week with works of art showing the events of each day of Holy Week.
See: www.cptryon.org/prayer/child/lent/holywk/index.html

4 Picturing Jesus picture packs
RE Today Services publishes four picture packs which include A4 laminated cards of paintings of the Easter story: *Picturing Jesus* (Packs A & B), *Picturing Jesus Fresh Ideas* and *Picturing Easter*.
See: http://shop.retoday.org.uk

5 Easter: a spiritual experience for the primary school
This article from *REtoday*, Spring 2007, shows a different set of activities used to create an Easter experience for children aged 7–11. It is available for free download for subscribers.
See: www.retoday.org.uk

6 Bring Easter alive: an Easter labyrinth
Further ideas for creating a labyrinth can be found in this unit by Pete Greaves in *Exploring a Theme: Celebrations*
See: http://shop.retoday.org.uk

7 Experiencing Easter
An imaginative approach to help children experience Easter using six easy-to-assemble, interactive stations set up in different parts of the church or school. Available from the Diocese of Gloucester.
See: www.gloucester.anglican.org

8 Easter journey
A series of scripts and suggested activities suitable for use in partnership with your local church to create a traditional Easter journey, sharing the story of Easter with children.
See: http://easterjourney.org.uk

What can children do as a result of this unit?

The following pupil friendly 'I can . . .' statements describe the learning that may be expected of pupils.

Level	Description of achievement: I can. . .
2	• suggest what is most important about the story of Easter • *respond sensitively to the story of Easter.*
3	• describe why Easter is one of the most important Christian festivals • *prepare an Easter experience reflecting on why Easter matters in Christianity, making a link to what matters to me.*
4	• explain how the story of Easter might help Christians to understand forgiveness • *apply ideas about forgiveness, struggle, suffering and hope for myself, referring to the story of Easter.*

Activity 1

Setting the scene

- **Explain** to the children that they are going to create an Easter experience for younger children.
- **Show** the children an online labyrinth, e.g. www.labyrinth.org.uk
- **Explain** that in medieval times pilgrims walked these labyrinths to spend time focusing on and praying to God. In modern times schools use labyrinths and reflection activities to find out more about different aspects of Christianity.
- **Ask:** Why do people walk labyrinths and take part in other reflections?
- **Show** the children extracts from the *Miracle Maker* DVD or **tell** them the story of the last week of Jesus' life using the pictures on page 22. This DVD from the Bible Society is an invaluable help to teaching about Jesus: see www.biblesociety.org.uk/miraclemaker
- **Ask:** What are the most important parts of the story?
- **Explain** to the children that over the next few lessons they are going to work in a group to present part of the Easter story and make a reflective activity to help another class think about what Easter means to Christians and what everyone can learn from the Easter story.

Activity 2

Creating the Easter experience

Organise the children into groups of 6–8, depending on the size of the class. Ideally the groups will have a mix of abilities. Then:

- **Decide** as a class which parts of the Holy Week story you are going to share within your Easter experience. How many parts of the story will you share?
- **Give** each group, or allow them to choose, a part of the story. The group needs to make sure they are familiar with their part of the story.
- **Ask** children to plan how they will share their story with the groups that come visit them, e.g. act the story out, read the story, show some pictures.

You will need to have a set of the activity cards cut out for each group to choose from.

Talk through each of the Easter experience activity cards with the class. Then ask groups to:

- **Explain** which activity goes best with which part of the story.
- **Choose** an activity from the cards that fits their story and which they will set up and run for another group.

Explain to the class where the Easter experience will take place e.g. in the local church or the school hall. Then:

- **Agree** how long each part of the Easter experience will last
- **Provide** time for each group to resource and practise their storytelling and the reflective activity.

Activity 3

Conducting the Easter experience

- **Venue:** Arrange a large space in which to set up the Easter experience. Plan this as a whole-day activity to allow for setting up and completing the experience. **Allow** children to set up their part of the Easter experience ensuring they have enough resources
- **Timing** will be important. One person in each group must be the time keeper to ensure all the visiting groups move between the activities at a similar time.
- **Supervision:** Each visiting group must be accompanied by an adult. Between each activity the adult can talk to the group about what they have learnt, allowing for all groups to be ready to start again at the same time.
- **Timetable:** The timetable might look like this.
  - · 20 minutes – Activity 1
  - · 5 minutes – discussion with group leader
  - · 20 minutes – Activity 2
  - · 5 minutes – discussion with group leader and so on
- **Reflection:** After the Easter experience there must be time for both those who visited the experience and those who created the experience to reflect.

A simple box structure allows space for words and illustrations from the children.

Today I was surprised by . . .	I found it hard to . . .
I think Easter is important to Christians because . . .	Today I have reflected on . . .

Alternative Activity 4

A teacher creates the Easter experience for children

The resources and instructions given on these pages will also support adults in creating an Easter experience for children. Note:

- You will need an adult to run each activity within the experience.
- Many schools have found that this is a good opportunity to liaise with their local church, who may allow you to conduct the experience in church and provide adults willing to help.

THE EASTER STORY

The triumphal entry into Jerusalem

The last supper

The Garden of Gethsemane and Peter's denial

The trial of Jesus

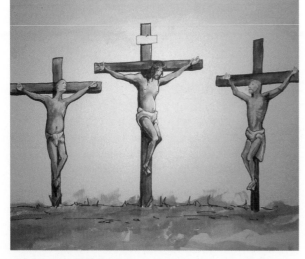

Jesus is crucified

Jesus' body is missing!

These images are available for subscribers to download from the RE Today website.

RE Today
Services

Activity cards

Activity suggestion 1   Visual focus

Provide the children engaging in your station with a series of pictures about your part of the story. Use them to help you tell your part of the story.

Ask them: *Which picture do they think shows the most important part of the story best? Why?*

Choose or adapt the activity below for your group to encounter.

Ask the children to:

- **work together** in pairs and choose one picture they would like to work with
- **choose** one child from each pair to stick a small sticky note with their face on it where they would most like to be in the picture
- **let the other child** in the pair ask a series of questions to help the first child think more deeply about the part of the Easter story they are focusing on, for example:

What exactly can you see?

What can you touch?

What can you hear, see, smell?

Who is nearest to you?

What are they thinking?

What would you say to them?

How would they reply?

What will happen in the next five minutes?

What are your own feelings?

What will you do next?

- **change roles**, letting each child take the other role in their pair.

Activity suggestion 2 Artistic focus

Choose an interesting way to share your part of the story with your group.

Show the children a selection of different types of crosses and explain the meaning of them.

Ask the children to:

- **create** a cross to be displayed either at a different time during Easter week or in a different location. Which places can you ask them to design a cross for?
- **decide** on a title for their cross and write a sentence to describe what it shows
- **tell** you where they would like to hang their cross and why.

Activity suggestion 3 Written focus

Choose an interesting way to share your part of the story with your group.

Explain to the children that during Easter week the followers of Jesus had lots of questions about what was happening and why it was happening. For Christians today what happened to Jesus at Easter answers questions about what happens when they die. Everyone asks lots of questions.

Ask the children to:

- **read** the following poem

- **write** a poem of their own that shows what their big questions about life are.

I wonder how

I wonder how the world is made?

I wonder how the birds fly?

I wonder how we grow?

I wonder what the deepest sea is?

I wonder why teachers are the boss?

I wonder why we die?

Madeline Knowles, aged 6

Activity suggestion 4 Finger labyrinth

Choose an interesting way to share your part of the story with your group.

Explain to the children that Christians believe that because Jesus died they can be forgiven for the bad choices that they make. Everyone makes bad choices.

Ask the children to:

- **make** a finger labyrinth or use the one shown.

- **follow** the labyrinth with a finger. When they get to the centre, think of one bad choice they have made and write or draw it and put it in the bin

- **follow** the labyrinth back out again.

Activity suggestion 5 Creative focus

Choose an interesting way to share your part of the story with your group.

Give your children the materials to make an Easter Garden that shows your part of the story. You will need to think carefully about what they will need to make the garden.

Ask the children to:

- **work together** as a group to make their garden. The garden should be suitable to display in a church

- **write** responses to the following sentence starters and display them in or around their garden.

  My special place is . . . because . . .

  Our Easter garden would be helpful to a Christian because . . .

Activity suggestion 6 Artistic focus

Provide the pupils engaging in your station with a series of pictures about your part of the story. Use them to help you tell your part of the story.

Ask the children to:

- **choose** one of the pictures to display in certain locations such as the school hall, an altar cloth, a bus poster advertising Easter celebrations or an art gallery

- **write** responses to some of the following sentence starters sharing their thoughts:

  I would put this picture . . . because . . .

  I would call this picture . . . because . . .

  I think Christians might like this picture because . . .

  I think Christians might find this picture difficult because . . .

RE Today
Services

Activity suggestion 7 Musical focus

Provide the children engaging in your station with a selection of pieces of music which could accompany your part of the story.

Ask the children to work in pairs to:

- **decide** which piece of music they think is most suitable for the part of the story you are focusing on, and say why

- **choose** a piece of music that would help a Christian think about the importance of this part of the Easter story

- **think** about a person in the story and **write** some words to describe their feelings.

Activity suggestion 8 Walking the labyrinth

A labyrinth is not like a maze. There is only one path to the centre and out again. Labyrinths were walked by medieval pilgrims as way of thinking about God.

Choose an interesting way to share your part of the story with your group.

You might:

- **mark out** a very simple labyrinth or path on the floor

- **create** four different activities for the children to take part in as they quietly and thoughtfully walk the labyrinth.

Use or adapt the activities below for your group to encounter. Each of the activities focuses on an aspect of the Easter story.

Struggling

The disciples struggled to understand why Jesus was killed. Jesus struggled to let himself be killed, even though he knew it had to happen.

- Think about something that you are finding hard or struggling with in your life.

- As you add a knot to the mess of strings in front you, think about who you can ask for help.

Saying sorry

Several people in the Easter story are sorry for things that they do, particularly Peter and Pilate.

- Write down something you are sorry for and then screw it up and put it in the bin.

- Wash your hands in the water to show that it is over and you won't do it again.

- Think about who you need to say sorry to.

Suffering

Jesus suffers in the Easter story and so do those who loved him. Everyone's life has some sad times.

- Take one of the heart shapes and write the name of someone who is having a sad time at the moment. Stick it onto the cross shape in front of you.

- Take another heart shape and write down something you could do to help that person. Put the heart in your pocket to take away.

Hope

For Christians the Easter story gives them hope that when they die they will go to live with God.

- Take one of the seeds and plant it with some soil in the pot.

- Stick a label on the side that completes the sentence:

  My hope for the future is . . .

WHAT DOES EASTER REALLY MEAN?
A focus on poetry

For the teacher

A quick Google image search on 'Easter' gives a very strong impression that Easter is all about bunnies, eggs, new lambs, spring flowers, and new life, with the story of the crucifixion and resurrection of Jesus struggling to find a place.

The activities in this section provide ways in for older pupils to grapple with some of the **big concepts** at the heart of Easter, e.g. **incarnation, forgiveness, hope, redemption, resurrection and salvation,** and to consider the **impact** of Easter on the everyday life of practising Christians today.

At the heart of these pages are **three poems,** and **two works of art**. The **five activities** described can be used flexibly, and ideally in a combination of two or more.

What can children do as a result of this unit?

The following pupil-friendly 'I can . . .' statements describe the learning that may be expected of pupils in the 10–11 age range.

Level	Description of achievement: I can. . .
3	• describe three things Christians believe in, and say what a difference the beliefs make at Easter
	• *prepare a reflection on the way resurrection matters at Easter in Christianity, making a link to what matters to me.*
4	• show that I understand how the Easter story can have an impact on Christians today
	• *create a statement of my own beliefs about God, Jesus and life after death, referring to ideas from the Christian story of Easter.*
5	• explain the impact, for a Christian, of believing that Jesus was crucified and rose from the dead
	• *express my own views about questions to do with life's meaning and purpose, taking account of ideas from the Christian story of Easter.*

See also:

1 **PoemHunter**
   PoemHunter provides a collection of poems to view online, including 'The Nail Man' by Steve Turner.
   See: www.poemhunter.com/poem/the-nail-man

2 **Stations of the Cross, Kenya**
   Lodwar Cathedral's website provides a virtual tour of 14 Stations of the Cross specially painted for the cathedral. Each station is accompanied by some (short) devotional text.
   See: www.edow.org/spirituality/lent/Kenya/stations.html

3 **Life of Jesus MAFA**
   The MAFA pictures illustrated on this website provide a coherent set of African illustrations of the gospel story.
   See: www.jesusmafa.com/anglais/accueil.htm

4 **Picturing Jesus picture packs**
   RE Today Services publishes four picture packs which include A4 laminated cards of paintings of the Easter story: *Picturing Jesus* (Packs A & B), *Picturing Jesus Fresh Ideas* and *Picturing Easter*.
   See: http://shop.retoday.org.uk

5 **Paul Cookson, poet**
   Paul Cookson's website presents Paul reading some of his favourite poems. Paul is a prolific writer and performer of poetry, both religious and secular. Many of his poems are written for a young audience. Why not invite him to your school?
   See: www.paulcooksonpoet.co.uk

6 **Spirited Arts and Spirited Poetry**
   Young people's entries to the two competitions published on this site provide excellent classroom stimulus.
   See: www.natre.org.uk/spiritedarts/index.php

7 ***Spirited Poetry: Reflections about Life, God and Faith,*** ed. Lat Blaylock, ISBN 978-1-85175-348-2

Curriculum links

Literacy: The activities link to the literacy framework for Year 6, enabling pupils to consider the use of personification and the effect of powerful images in poetry, and providing an opportunity for pupils to write their own poetry.

Spiritual development: by learning about and reflecting on aspects of the Easter story and its impact on the everyday lives of Christians.

Easter poems

Only at Easter

Whips circled and crudely landed
to lash life out of him,
or so it appeared.
Spikes were summoned
to close the stone vault,
and the sky growled.
Haughty robes of passing power
flapped through women wailing,
towards, unknowingly, the chasm of pride,
the parched well of no comfort.
How much those perished priests,
Like us, didn't know.

Rising, he rose.
Risen, he remains.
His remains, apart from some ruby drops,
he took with him.
They became our passport out of death,
our living ascent from a
lifeless climate.
His scent of wounds,
in which we are now wrapped,
carried us out of that petrified place
into the calm city
where even the dust has been healed.

© Stewart Henderson, 1989. From
A Giant's Scrapbook by Stewart Henderson
(Hodder & Stoughton, 1989).
Used with permission of Hodder & Stoughton Ltd.

I don't believe in Easter

I don't believe in Easter.
I don't believe in celebrating cuddly little bunny
rabbits.
I don't believe in celebrating fluffy cute day old chicks.
I don't believe in celebrating sugary sweet chocolate
eggs.
I don't believe in celebrating decorated flowery
bonnets.

But I do believe in celebrating the Truth of the
Easter Story.
All year round.

© Paul Cookson, 2009. From *Let No One Steal Your Dreams* by
Paul Cookson (Twist in the Tale, 2009).
Used with permission of the author.
See www.paulcooksonpoet.co.uk.

The Nail Man

Which one was it
that held the nails
and then hammered them
into place?

Did he hit them
out of anger,
or a simple
sense of duty?

Was it a job
that had to be done,
or a good day's work
in the open air?

And when they
clawed past bone
and bit into wood,
was it like all the others,
or did history
shudder a little
beneath the head
of that hammer?

Was he still there,
packing away his tools,
when 'It is finished'
was uttered to the throng,
or was he at home
washing his hands
and getting ready
for the night?

Will he be
among the forgiven
on that Day of Days,
his sin having been slain
by his own savage spike?

© 2002 Steve Turner. From *Poems* by Steve Turner
(Lion Hudson, 2002).
Used with permission of Lion Hudson plc.

Activities

Activity 1 — Googling Easter

Pupils work in pairs or small groups and need internet access.

Ask pupils to:

- **investigate** the results of a Google image search on the word 'Easter'. What do they notice? What might someone who has never heard of Easter assume it was about, if this was their only source?

- **read** Paul Cookson's poem 'I don't believe in Easter' (page 27). **Explain** what they think he means, and **suggest** what else is needed to understand what Easter is about for Christians.

- **invite** people from the local Christian faith community to visit the class to talk and answer questions about what Easter means to them and the impact it has on their everyday life.

- **write** a poem following the structure of 'I don't believe in Easter' expressing what they do – and don't – believe in.

Activity 2 — Engaging with poetry

Pupils work in small groups, with a copy of page 27 and the six definitions of concepts from page 29.

Ask pupils to:

- **listen** to the three poems on page 27 being read to them several times, and **read** the poems for themselves in their group. **Clarify** the meaning of any words they are unsure of.

- **identify** examples of personification and powerful images in the poems (e.g. 'the sky growled'; 'did history shudder') and **talk about** the effectiveness of this use of language. What mood does it create? What questions does it raise? How does it affect their understanding of the message the poet is trying to convey?

- **make links** between the six definitions of Christian concepts on page 29 and words and phrases in the poems.

- **reflect on** how each poem helps to explain what Christians believe about Easter. Which poem does this most effectively, and why?

- **decide** which poem would be most suitable to be read in each of the following situations, and **explain** why: assembly for Year 4; church service; funeral service; TV programme about different ways of celebrating Easter. Compare answers with other groups – which poem was most/last chosen for each situation? Why?

Then move on to Activity 3 or 4.

Activity 3 — Responding to Easter poems

Ask pupils, working individually or in pairs/small groups, to choose one of the following ways of responding personally to the Easter theme of the poems they have read.

1 **Write a poem or make a collage** to express why Easter is important to Christians. Pupils could start off by recording their own ideas quickly, and then share them with the class. The class could work together to select the best lines/images/ideas, and then individuals work with the selection to create their own poem or collage.

2 **Write a poem** from the perspective of one of the people or items taking part or observing the action, e.g. Mary, the soldier, the hammer, the cross. Provide suggestions for the type of poem, or the structure, and also for opportunities to read/perform the finished piece.

3 **Dance the poem**: Pupils work individually or with others to create and perform a dance inspired by one of the poems. Colours, movements and fabrics can all be used to reflect the mood, message and impact of Easter on Christians.

4 **Compose (or choose) a piece of music** to accompany one of the poems on page 27 or a poem written by the pupil. NATRE's resource 'Developing RE through music' provides a vast collection of online music clips arranged according to some 60 themes found in RE. Pupils might find this useful as a starting point for their own composition or selection.

See: www.natre.org.uk/music

Activity 4 — Celebrating Easter all year round

> But I do believe in celebrating the Truth of the Easter Story.
>
> All year round.

These are the closing words of Paul Cookson's poem 'I don't believe in Easter' (page 25). This activity asks pupils to work with, and show their understanding of, the idea that for Christians the message of Easter is relevant to the whole year, not just the days around Holy Week and Easter Day.

Ask pupils, working in small groups, to plan an Easter assembly to take place in October.

They could consider:

- the key message of the assembly, e.g. the impact of the message of Easter on Christians today

- poems, stories, prayers

- music, dance, artwork

- visitors – e.g. from the local Christian faith community.

Ask groups to share their plans, and give reasons for their choices and decisions. If possible, provide an opportunity for the assembly to be delivered.

RE Today Services

Twelfth Station: Jesus dies on the cross

Painted by artists from Turkana, Kenya, around 1995 and housed in Lodwar Cathedral in Kenya.

See: www.edow.org/spirituality/lent/Kenya/stations.html

Reproduced by kind permission of St Patrick's Missionary Society (photograph by Fr Martin Smith SPS).

Working in a small group, look carefully at the two pictures on this page, and decide together your responses to the questions below.

1 Which people from the gospel story can you see? How do you know?

2 What similarities and differences between the two pictures can you see? Which picture do you prefer, and why?

3 If you have access to the internet, check out the website of Lodwar Cathedral (see left) and find out about the background to the picture. Then click on number 12, and read the short prayer which accompanies the picture. Why is the word 'we' used?

4 Look at the six Christian beliefs in boxes at the bottom of this page. Check you understand what they mean, and then for each picture choose the belief which you think would work best as a caption for each picture. Explain your choice.

5 If you were to draw/design your own 'crucifixion' picture, what would it be like? Do a quick sketch to capture your ideas and explain them to your group.

Share your group's ideas with the rest of the class. What similarities and differences do you notice? What surprises you?

La Crucifixion by Bernard Buffet, 1951 Reproduced by kind permission of the artist.

Incarnation	Forgiveness	Hope
Christians believe Jesus was an ordinary human person, but at the same time he was truly 'God on earth'.	Jesus taught people to forgive even an enemy. He showed them how, then he did it himself, from his cross.	Even though the world is a mess, Christians believe that Jesus brings hope for the future on earth and in heaven. Jesus proved the possibility of hope in many ways.
Redemption	**Inspiration**	**Strength**
Christians believe that Jesus wasn't just an ordinary person. He was sent by God to redeem the world from our own bad choices and from evil.	Some people have a capacity to inspire, excite and motivate others. People want to be with them and follow them. Jesus did this.	Christians think that Jesus was strong because he was in touch with God. He used his strength to help others, not for selfish reasons.

Making progress: learning about Easter and learning from Easter

For the teacher

Easter is a topic that is often studied annually in RE, or at least several times during the primary years. This recurrence lends itself to an increasing depth of understanding of its significance and to building up skills through differentiated tasks.

The **progression grid** on page 31 shows seven increasingly challenging things you might do with your pupils 4–11 years of age that build learning power about Easter.

- The chart describes the achievements of pupils across the age range in terms drawn from the English eight-level RE scale, working up from Early Learning Goals to Level 5.
- Where in the progression grid we talk about 'the story of Holy Week and Easter', we mean the series of events around Jesus' last days. 'Holy Week' is the time from Palm Sunday to Good Friday. Easter itself begins properly on Easter Sunday or Saturday night after midnight.

Telling the story

The telling of the story needs to be age appropriate but even when sharing the story with younger children there are **six key parts of the story** which should not be left out:

- Jesus' triumphant entry into Jerusalem – celebrated as Palm Sunday
- Throwing the moneychangers out of the temple – this shows one reason Jesus had enemies
- Sharing bread and wine at the Last Supper – a way to remember Jesus
- Judas and the guards – a false friend and the arrest of Jesus in the Garden of Gethsemane
- The trial and death of Jesus –Jesus' forgiveness of his killers
- The empty tomb and the story of Jesus rising again – the mystery of what happened and the Christian belief that God raised Jesus to life again.

Telling the story, using the objects

There are numerous excellent retellings of the stories available, but the best one for your class is probably the one you prepare yourself. One way of doing this is to use some artefacts and symbols to connect the different parts of the story. You could start these activities at almost any age group by playing 'Kim's Game', in which the pupils look for one minute at a tray with these objects on it, then try to remember them all. Your tray might have on it:

- A palm leaf
- A plastic donkey
- A small bag of coins
- A piece of bread
- A bowl of water
- A small towel
- A glass of red wine
- A round stone
- A nail
- A prickly branch woven into a circle
- A hot cross bun
- A jar of ointment

- A toy spear

Vary the objects, and have more for older children. When you bring the tray back into view, see how many the children remember.

Ask:

- Which one connects to each part of the story? How and why?
- Which ones are the most important reminders for Christians of their beliefs about Jesus?

Teaching Easter across the primary school: a progression grid

	Teaching and learning activity suggestions	So that they might be able to . . .	And work at levels . . .
4–5 year olds	**Three interesting artefacts** • After hearing the stories of Jesus from Holy Week and Easter, pupils see, hear about and handle three Christian artefacts – a palm cross, a crucifix and an empty cross. • They talk about which one is the 'odd one out' (any of the three could be for different reasons).	**Recall** the story and say what they think about some objects linked to Holy Week and Easter.	**Level 1/Early Learning Goals** I can remember and talk about three things about the Easter story.
5–6 year olds	**Bread, wine, buns and gardens** • Children explore the symbols of bread and wine, hot cross buns and an Easter Garden. • They draw lines of connection on labelled diagrams (as in literacy – 'labels lists and captions') to connect the symbols, parts of the story and suggested meanings.	**Connect** a symbol with a part of the story or a memory. Identify a meaning in a symbol.	**Level 2** I can identify some features of Easter and suggest meanings in the religious story.
6–7 year olds	**Feelings from the story** From the story of Holy Week and Easter children think/pair/share two moments that go with particular feelings • two happy moments • two puzzling moments • two sad moments • two moments of strength for Jesus (there are good SEAL links here).	**Say** which of the two moments is happier, more puzzling and so on. **Link** their own emotions to the emotions of the story.	**Level 2** I can identify meanings in the story and respond sensitively to questions about feelings and experiences.
7–8 year olds	**Six emotions of mine** • Before listening to the story of Holy Week and Easter, children give six examples of when they were excited, worried, puzzled, cross, very upset and hopeful. They link their emotions to the disciples' emotions in the stories. • They begin to connect the emotions of the story with their own stories of life.	**Express** their ideas about the emotions of Good Friday and Easter Sunday in designs and captions for two greetings cards.	**Level 3** I can make links between my own attitudes and the disciples' feelings in the stories of Holy Week and Easter, thinking for myself.
8–9 year olds	**Text/art/music** • Compare short extracts of Bible texts with some of the artwork and/or music that Christians use at Easter. How have the artists used the texts or the story? • Make a song or a work of art of their own from one verse of the Bible story. How are they using the texts?	**Link up** different forms of spiritual expression (text, music, art) and make links to their own responses to the story.	**Level 3** I can connect the ways Christians express their ideas about Holy Week and Easter with some ideas of my own.
9–10 year olds	**What matters at Easter today?** • Investigate Holy Week and Easter in a local Christian community, making a list of 'Ten important parts of the festival'. Rank the list, saying what matters most to Christians in Easter celebrations. • Make a list of ten things that matter in their own family life, and compare.	**Develop** their skills and understanding through thinking skills and investigations of their own, comparing reasons for what matters.	**Level 4** I can show I understand the sources of Easter celebration, and their practices, and apply ideas about celebration to my own life.
10–11 year olds	**Eucharist: Remembering Jesus worldwide** Pupils enquire into the practice of Eucharist/ Holy Communion in a modern Christian community. They might ask: • Why do Christians in hundreds of countries use wine and bread to remind them of Jesus? • What music, art and words do they use, and why? The focus on remembering Jesus leads to a consideration of what memories are most important, and why.	**Explain** some ways that Eucharist relates to Jesus' last supper, and consider the significance of bread and wine, relating this to their own ideas about remembrance.	**Level 5** I can explain clearly connections between modern Christian worship and ancient story, and express my views about a spiritual question such as 'What should always be remembered?'

Four key aspects of teaching Christian festivals

When planning to teach about any Christian festival it is helpful to consider four key aspects.

1 Events

The complex events of this historic but still religiously significant period need to be clearly explained to pupils to avoid the idea that Jesus was born at Christmas and died four months later. Page 2 provides a list of where the significant parts of the story can be found in Luke's gospel. Discuss with the children why these events are still significant for Christians 2000 years after the events occurred.

2 Customs

This area can be over-done in schools, leaving no time to consider the significance of Easter for Christians. Well-meaning schools run egg-decorating competitions and Easter parades, but is this balanced with progressed teaching of beliefs? Ensure pupils can discern between secular and Christian ways of celebrating Easter. Schools that want to look at Christian customs may want to start with Shrove Tuesday and Ash Wednesday and move to the outdoor performances telling the story of Holy Week that are performed in several cities on Good Friday.

See: http://citc.dioceseofleicester.com/?page_id=19

3 Experience

The external features of what believers do to celebrate or remember key aspects of the story are particularly important at Easter as they track the emotions of the story and the significance of the beliefs behind the celebration. Sharing the difference between the music used on Palm Sunday (or Maundy Thursday or Good Friday) and Easter Sunday is one way of showing this. The article on page 20 allows pupils to reflect on part of the Christian experience of Easter.

4 Beliefs

The central beliefs of Easter are complex and profound:

- **Incarnation** – the belief that God became human in Jesus.

- **Forgiveness** – the belief that when people are sorry for the sins they commit they will be forgiven by God.

- **Hope** – the belief that Jesus brings hope that life on earth can be better and that there is life after death, with God.

- **Resurrection** – the belief that Jesus rose from the dead on the third day after his death by crucifixion; also the rising from the dead of believers on the Last Day.

- **Salvation** – the belief that through the death of Jesus people are saved from the eternal consequences of sin.

See also: www.request.org.uk

These four aspects of festival are shown in the chart below applied to Easter.

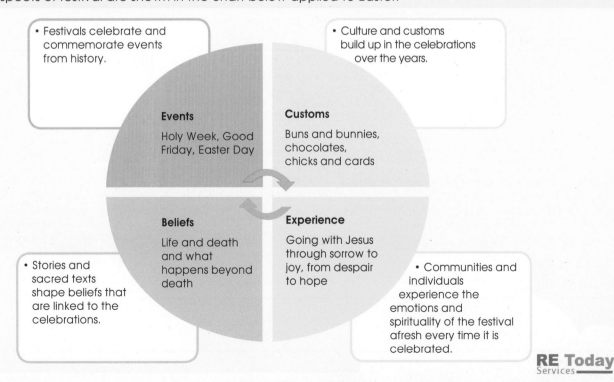

- Festivals celebrate and commemorate events from history.

- Culture and customs build up in the celebrations over the years.

Events

Holy Week, Good Friday, Easter Day

Customs

Buns and bunnies, chocolates, chicks and cards

Beliefs

Life and death and what happens beyond death

Experience

Going with Jesus through sorrow to joy, from despair to hope

- Stories and sacred texts shape beliefs that are linked to the celebrations.

- Communities and individuals experience the emotions and spirituality of the festival afresh every time it is celebrated.

RE Today
Services